BrAiN BENDERS

SEEING IS BELIEVING

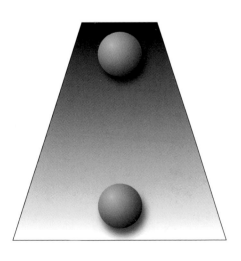

Thanks to the creative team:

Senior Editor: Alice Peebles

Designer: Bryony Anne Warren and Collaborate Agency

First American edition published in 2015 by Lerner Publishing Group, Inc.

Hungry Tomato™
A division of Lerner Publishing Group, Inc.
241 First Avenue North
Minneapolis, MN 55401 USA

For reading levels and more information, look up this title
at www.lernerbooks.com.

Library of Congress Cataloging-in-Publication Data

Moore, Gareth, 1975–
    Seeing is believing / by Dr. Gareth Moore.
        pages cm. — (Brain benders)
    ISBN 978-1-4677-6345-5 (lb : alk. paper) — ISBN 978-1-4677-7201-3
(pb: alk. paper) — ISBN 978-1-4677-7202-0 (eb pdf)
    1. Optical illusions—Juvenile literature. 2. Visual perception—Juvenile
literature. I. Title.
QP495.M67 2016
152.14'8—dc23   2015001584

Manufactured in the United States of America
1 – VP – 7/15/15

SEEING IS BELIEVING

by Dr. Gareth Moore

HUNGRY TOMATO™

MINNEAPOLIS

Contents

Seeing Is Believing

Can you believe your eyes? Normally you can, but sometimes they'll lie to you! Get ready to be amazed by just how confused your brain can become! Prepare for patterns that move, colors that change, and objects that shift in size. Explore these optical illusions with some help from the tips at the back of the book, and check out the answers to learn what makes each puzzle work. You won't believe your eyes!

Negative image

Look at some of the red dots in this box, and move your eyes around from dot to dot. You should see not only the red dots, but also ghostly after-images. These linger behind in your eyes and appear as extra, bright dots in the empty spaces. They might also be light blue in color.

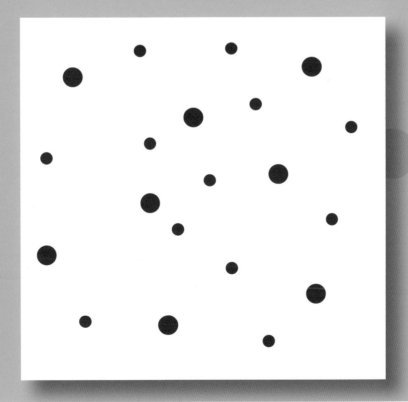

Need help with solving these puzzles? Turn to pages 26 – 29 for helpful tips.

Introducing Illusions

Can you always believe your eyes? Sometimes they have trouble making sense of what they're seeing – as you're about to find out!

1 Moving around

Hold the book very close to your face and look at the center of this pattern. Now slowly move the book away from you, while still looking at the center. The different curves start to swirl around, as if they were moving on the page!

2 Parallel problem

These blue and orange lines look as if they get farther apart or closer together as they run across the page, but is that true? Test this out by using a ruler to measure the distance between an orange line and a blue line at the top of the picture, and again at the bottom.

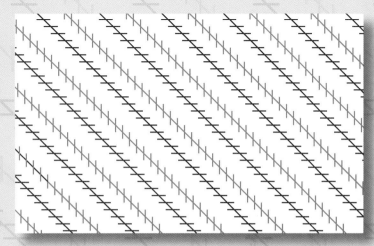

3 Lining up

If this white line were to continue in the same direction, which of the colored lines would it meet up with? Take a guess using just your eyes, then find out the answer by using a ruler. Were you right?

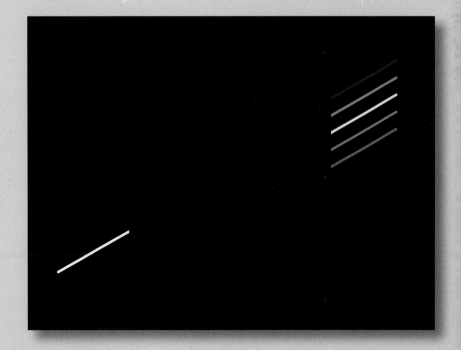

Need help with solving these puzzles? Turn to pages 26 – 29 for helpful tips.

Misleading Measurements

When you look at two different objects, can you always tell which is larger and which is smaller? Are you sure? These optical illusions might surprise you!

1 Circle size

Which of these two green circles is larger? Take a look first. Then, once you've decided, measure them.

2 Rectangle comparison

Which of the three green rectangles is exactly the same size as the vertical yellow rectangle? Again, decide first, then measure them.

3 | Tabletop teaser

If you look at these red tabletops, they seem to be very different shapes – but would you believe that they are in fact identical? They are both exactly the same parallelogram. See if you can confirm this by using a ruler. It's surprising, isn't it?

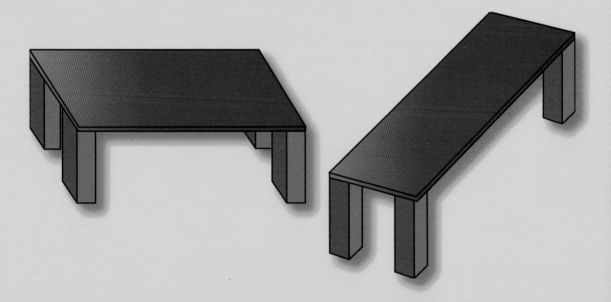

4 | Pointing apart

Which pair of arrow points do you think is farther apart – the left-hand and middle ones or the middle and right-hand ones?

Need help with solving these puzzles? Turn to pages 26 – 29 for helpful tips.

Distance Illusions

Your brain uses your eyes to figure out how far away objects are. It does this by comparing the view from one eye with the view from the other. But your brain also uses other cues to help it estimate distances. The illusions on this page demonstrate some of the visual decoding techniques that you use every day without realizing it!

1 Bowling balls

Look at these two blue bowling balls. Does the one at the top look larger? Try measuring them both to find out.

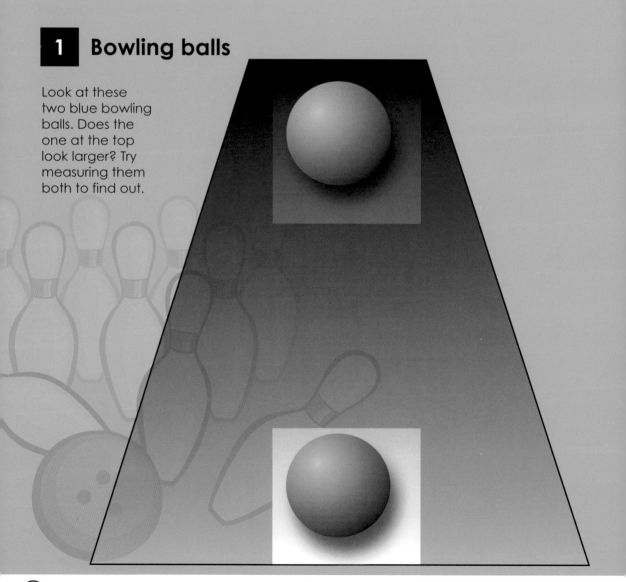

2 Railway line

There are two wide bars on top of these railroad tracks, but the one at the top looks much larger than the one at the bottom. Measure them both to find out if all is as it seems.

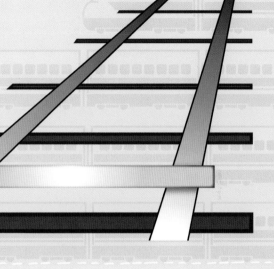

3 Salt and pepper

This photograph appears to show one large shaker and one small shaker, but it's actually two shakers of exactly the same size. The picture hasn't been changed since it was taken, so can you work out how the photographer made the shakers look like they are different sizes?

Need help with solving these puzzles? Turn to pages 26 – 29 for helpful tips.

Two-in-One Illusions

Seeing is believing, but what if you can see things that aren't even there? Your eyes are very good at noticing familiar patterns, so sometimes even empty spaces can look like objects. Your brain is also great at spotting faces, which is why you can sometimes see what looks like a face on the surface of the moon!

1 Face the vase

What do you see here? Is it a vase? Or is it two people looking at each other?

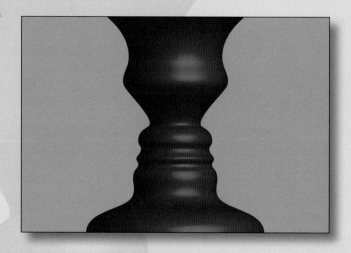

2 Hair or no hair?

Is this a man with a moustache and lots of hair?

Or is it a bald man with a beard? Can you find him, too?

3 Pointing both ways

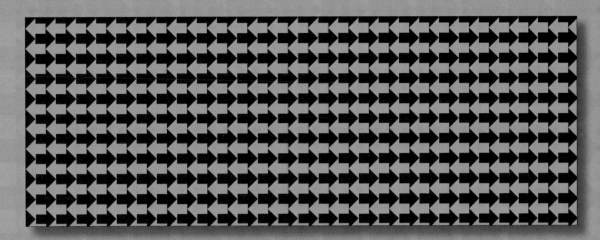

Do you see orange arrows pointing to the left, or blue arrows pointing to the right?

4 Soda or glasses?

Is this a few shelves of glasses, or a collection of soda bottles?

Need help with solving these puzzles? Turn to pages 26 – 29 for helpful tips.

Context Illusions

How you see an object in the real world depends not just on the object itself, but also on the appearance of everything around it. The illusions on these pages show this in three different ways.

1 Whiteout

Looking at this picture at normal reading distance, you see a swirl of white lines heading off into blackness.

But focus on the center of the picture, then slowly move the page closer, and something strange happens.

The white area in the center expands, becoming both larger and brighter.

2 Whiter than white

The white square in the center of each of these black squares appears to be glowing a much brighter white than the rest of the paper. But can that really be true?

3 Side by side

The path on the right of this picture seems to head off at a different angle from the path on the left.

Or is this just an optical illusion?

Need help with solving these puzzles? Turn to pages 26 – 29 for helpful tips.

Color Perception

We all know that colors look very different at night than during the day, and have you ever noticed how different indoor lights can have a big effect on what a color looks like? It's not just the type of light bulb in a lamp that changes a color, though. Did you know that other nearby colors can also influence how you see light, shade, and color?

1 Gray areas

Look at these columns of gray discs. There appear to be two different shades of gray: light gray and dark gray. But is that really true? Are you sure?

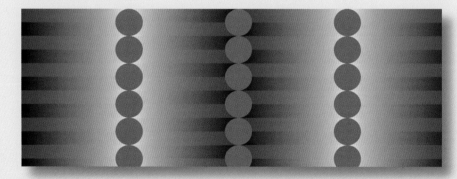

2 Shades of color

There seem to be three different shades of these four different colors here, but in fact something strange is happening.

The black and white bars are changing your color perception. Take a closer look and see if you can figure out what's going on!

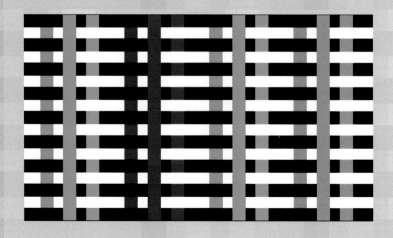

3 Colored lights

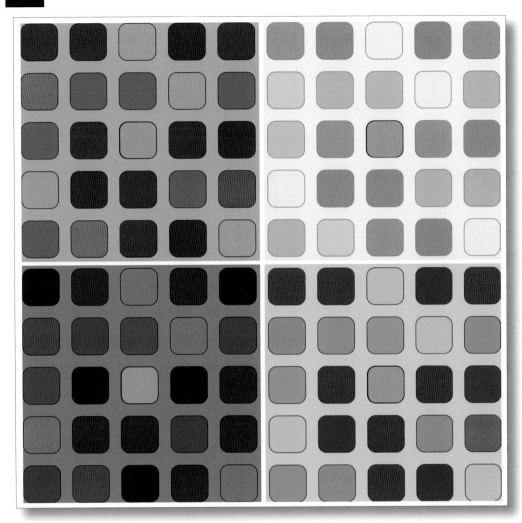

Look at the center tile in each of these four colored areas. In the top left picture, the center tile appears pale green, and in the top right picture it looks pale blue.

In the bottom left picture it seems to be yellow, and in the bottom right picture it seems to be a pale purple color. But are the colors actually varying?

Try comparing each of these center tiles with this single grey tile. Surely they can't all be the same color ... or can they?

Need help with solving these puzzles? Turn to pages 26 – 29 for helpful tips.

Color Shifts

Things that you think you can see probably often surprise you, because they turn out to be just your imagination. You might see imagined details even with simple shapes, as the illusions on these pages will show you. You'll find that your eyes can also choose to hide details that really are there!

1 Color flood

Take a look at this shape, and compare the paper inside this shape with the paper just outside the shape. Is the paper in the center a slightly different shade from what you see outside the shape?

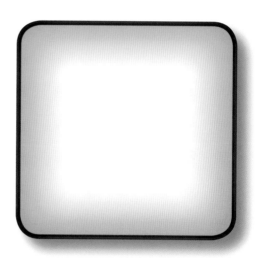

2 Boundary issues

Look at this green circle with a black cross on it. Does the whole circle look exactly the same shade of green Are you sure?

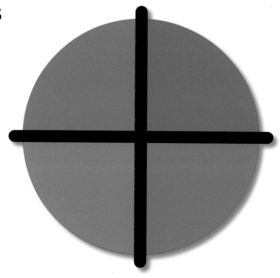

3 | Simulating shapes

Do you see a pale orange square in the center of this picture?

Does the paper there look a slightly different color?

And can you even see some of the edges of that square?

How about these green circles? Some parts are missing, but can you see a bright white hexagon in the middle?

You might even see a three-dimensional cube, too, if your brain is really creative!

Look at these blue circles, each with a quarter colored red. Can you also see a red square on the paper between them?

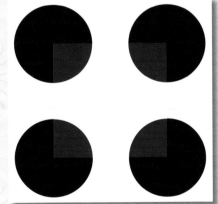

Need help with solving these puzzles? Turn to pages 26 – 29 for helpful tips.

Inversion Illusions

Have you ever looked at a bright light and found that your eyes didn't work so well afterward? You see a ghostly image of the bright light, like a large spot on your vision. The brighter the light and the longer you look at it, the stronger the effect. If you stare at a really bright light, like the sun, you can damage your eyesight permanently – so never look directly at the sun!

It's not just bright lights that can cause a ghostly image. Looking at the same image for a long time, without moving your eyes, can do the same. In both cases, your eyes have been looking at the same picture for so long that it takes them a while to forget about it. What you see afterward is the "opposite" of that picture, which is why a bright white light becomes a black spot in your vision.

1 Target rings

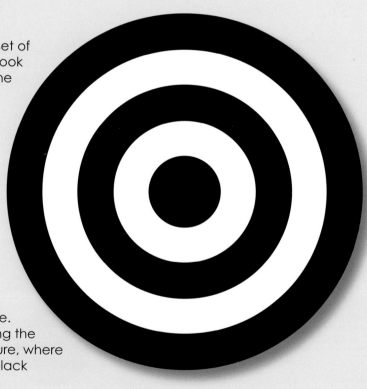

Stare into the center of this set of circles for 10 seconds, then look away at a white wall or at the ceiling. What do you see?

You should see a floating set of circles, similar to this image. Stare right into the center of these floating circles. This will make them easier to see, and after a second or two you will see the whole image even more clearly.

Did you notice that the middle circle is now empty? It isn't black like in the picture. This is because you are seeing the opposite of the original picture, where white becomes black and black becomes white.

2 Traffic lights

The same effect also works with color. Try staring at the center circle in this set of three for 20 seconds, then look away at a something far away and white, like a wall. What do you see?

Can you see different colors appearing? You should be able to see the three colors of traffic lights – red at the top, yellow in the middle, and green at the bottom.

If you only see one or two of these colors, that's OK too.

3 Coloring transmission

Stare at the black dot in the center of the first picture for 20 seconds. Then look immediately at the black dot in the center of the gray picture below. Try to do this without blinking!

What do you see? Does the gray image now appear in color? What color is the background? What about each of the shapes? They are not the same as in the upper image. The effect vanishes if you blink or take too long to move your eyes to the second black dot, so try again if you don't see it the first time!

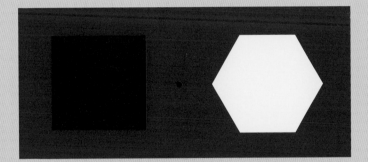

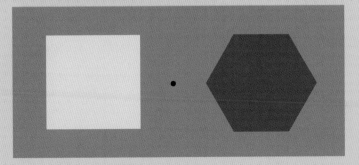

Need help with solving these puzzles? Turn to pages 26 – 29 for helpful tips.

21

Grid Illusions

Even fairly simple drawings often cause you to see far-from-simple illusions. The drawings on this page are extra simple – not much more than regular grids, just like you would find on a piece of graph paper!

1 Shape in the hole

This simple square grid has gaps where the lines would otherwise cross.

There's nothing special about these gaps – but there appears to be a bright white circle in every one of them!

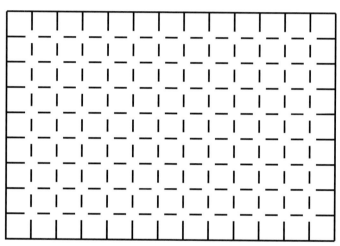

2 Colored circles

In this picture the missing parts of the lines have been put back in, but they have been drawn in color rather than black.

Amazingly, you can still see circles where the gaps were before, but now they take on the color used to fill in the gaps!

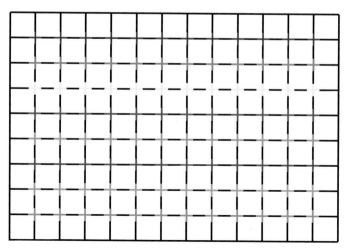

3 | Ghostly dots

This very simple drawing of blue squares on a black background hides some ghostly gray dots. Look at any of the blue squares, and then move your eyes to look at a different square. You will see gray dots flickering on the intersections between squares, just beyond the center of your vision.

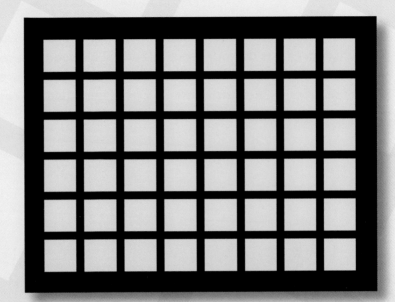

4 | More ghostly dots

This picture shows a regular grid of green lines on a black background. Where the grid lines intercept, there's a pale dot.

That's all there is to the picture, and yet as you move your eyes around it, you will see black dots flashing randomly on and off on top of each of the pale dots!

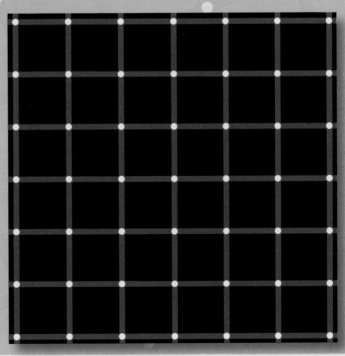

Need help with solving these puzzles? Turn to pages 26 – 29 for helpful tips.

Persistence of Vision

Your eyes can remember what they've seen for a short period of time, even after the picture itself has disappeared. This effect is called "persistence of vision," and it's how film and television work. Those images aren't really moving. They're just a lot of still images that flash past your eyes very quickly. Your eyes can also get tired and stop telling you about things they think you already know.

1 Negative image

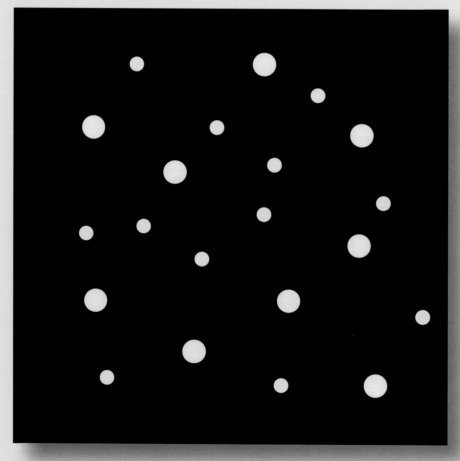

As you did on page 5, look at these yellow dots, then move your eyes around from dot to dot. What do you see now?

2 Fade to gray

Hold the book so this gray circle fills most of your vision, and stare at the center, making sure you don't move your eyes away.

After just a second or two, you should find that the entire circle fades until you can't see it at all!

Moving your eyes around will make it appear again.

3 Vanishing colors

There are five brightly colored shapes in this image. Hold the book as close as you can while still being able to see them all. Now focus on the orange shape in the center. Stare into the middle of it and you will find that the four other colored shapes vanish!

Keep staring and eventually the orange shape will fade away, too.

Need help with solving these puzzles? Turn to pages 26 – 29 for helpful tips.

Helpful Tips

Page 5

Seeing Is Believing

If you don't see this immediately, try looking at each dot for a little longer.

Pages 6 – 7

Introducing Illusions

Moving around

Notice that if you focus on a corner of the image instead of on the center, the swirling effect lessens.

Parallel problem

Arrange two pieces of paper very close together on top of the image, so that you can only see a small part of the image in between. Now slide the pieces of paper up and down the image. Do the lines still seem to move apart?

Lining up

Once you've made up your mind, rotate the book and look along the length of the white line. What do you think now?

Pages 10 – 11

Distance Illusions

Bowling balls

When something moves farther away from you, it appears to get smaller. In this drawing, the background creates an illusion of distance, so cover over as much of the gray shape as you can and look just at the two balls.

Railway line

It looks like the railroad is heading off into the distance, so if this were a photograph, you'd know that the upper bar would actually have to be much bigger for it appear the same size as the other bar. Try covering over some of the rails. What happens now?

Salt and pepper

If the shakers are the same size and the photograph is real, the trick is in the way they were photographed. To get this result, what angle would you need to photograph the shakers from?

Pages 8 – 9

Misleading Measurements

Circle size

Similar objects are often similar sizes, so this illusion relies on your brain assuming that all the red circles are related in size in some way. If you cover the red circles, what do you think now?

Rectangle comparison

Try rotating the book as you concentrate on just the top two rectangles.

Tabletop teaser

Cover the table legs and see what you think now.

Pointing apart

Your brain assumes it should be looking at the arrows' centers to judge how far apart they are. but it's actually the arrow tips that matter. Try covering most of each arrow so that you can just see the tip of each.

Pages 12 – 13 Two-in-One Illusions

Face the vase

If you focus on the blue area in the middle, what do you see? Now focus on on the orange background. Notice something else?

Hair or no hair?

Did you find the bearded man? Have you tried looking at the picture from a different angle?

Pointing both ways

The gaps between the drawn arrows make identical arrow shapes pointing the opposite way. You can try drawing this yourself. Can you come up with other patterns that work like this?

Soda or glasses?

The gaps between the glasses really do look like shelves and bottles. You might see the glasses first because they are shaded to look like real objects. But even with this visual cue, you can still see the bottles if you choose.

Pages 14 – 15 Context Illusions

Whiteout

Move the book toward you more slowly. Make sure you stay focused on the very center of the image. As you change what you can see in your peripheral vision, your vision adapts to the parts of the image it can still see.

Whiter than white

To find out if this is an illusion, try hiding

the black squares to see if they're causing the effect.

One way to do this is to take another piece of paper and cut a small hole in it. Lay it on the page and use the hole to look at different white parts of the picture.

Side by side

Try covering over one path, then covering over the other. Now what do you think?

Page 16
Color Perception

Gray areas

Take a piece of paper and place it over the drawing. Now put a small X over a light gray circle, and another small X over a dark gray circle. Remove the paper and cut out a small hole at each X. Put the paper back in place and look through the holes. Do they still seem to be different shades of gray?

Shades of color

Place two pieces of paper close together, leaving only a very narrow gap between them. Lay them on the page so that you can see just one of the black strips, revealing two shades of each color. Do they still look like different shades? Now slide the pieces of paper down so that you can see just one of the white strips, again revealing two shades of each color. Do they still look like they are different shades, too?

Page 17
Color Perception

Colored lights

Make a small hole in a plain piece of paper and look through it at each of the center tiles as well as the single gray tile.

Page 18
Color Shifts

Color flood

If you have trouble seeing this, give your eyes a rest. Then try again later in different light.

Color part of the edge to match the green on the page as closely as you can, using colored pencils or crayons. Next, move the paper's edge over each of the other quarters in turn. Do they all match the color in the same way?

Boundary issues

Place the edge of a piece of paper over one of the quarters of the circle.

Page 19
Color Shifts

Simulating shapes

If you have trouble seeing these hidden shapes, try looking at the book in brighter light. They are much harder to see in low lighting.

Pages 20 – 21

Inversion Illusions

Target rings

If you don't see the floating circles, look at the picture for twice as long and in a brighter light, and decide in advance where you will look afterward.

Traffic lights

If you don't see anything, try using a piece of bright white paper instead of a distant wall. If you just see a blur, focus directly on the center of that ghostly image. This will help you see it more clearly.

Coloring transmission

Make sure to look only at the black dots and nowhere else, and try not to blink! If you still can't see it, look at the color image for longer before you switch to the gray and white image.

Grid Illusions

Shape in the hole

To see the circles, try staring directly at the gaps.

Ghostly dots

Look at a blue square and then slowly relax your eyes. As you soften your focus, you should see the ghostly dots more clearly.

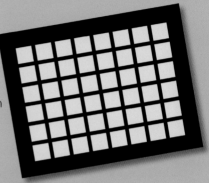

Colored circles

Look directly at the yellow crosses, since they provide the most visual contrast with the black lines.

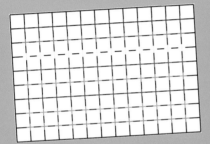

More ghostly dots

If you don't see these, move your eyes around slightly more quickly, or look out of the corners of your eyes at the rest of the grid. You can also try holding the book a little closer to you.

Persistence of Vision

Negative image

You can still see this effect even if you don't look directly at the dots.

Look at the background in one place for a second or so. Then shift your gaze to another part of the background.

Fade to gray

If you have trouble seeing this effect, head to a brighter room and hold the book a little closer. If this still doesn't work, put the book down for a bit and try again later – maybe your eyes are getting too tired!

Vanishing colors

This effect works best with bright, even lighting, so make sure there are no shadows on the page and that you are holding the book as still as you can.

Answers

Page 6–7 Introducing Illusions

Moving around

This image is hard for your eyes to focus on, so they move around rapidly, creating an impression of movement.

Parallel problem

The lines are all perfectly parallel. None of them get any closer together or farther apart at any point in the picture.

Lining up

The white line points at the blue line.

Pages 10 – 11 Distance Illusions

Bowling balls

The balls are identical in size. The upper part of the gray shape appears to be farther away, so your brain assumes that the upper ball must be larger than the lower ball. This illusion works because the farther away an object is, the smaller it appears to your eyes. Your brain automatically corrects for this, so you don't get confused by objects appearing to change size as you move around the world. But here, the top of the shape isn't really farther away from you, so your brain gets it wrong when it tells you the upper ball is larger than it actually is.

Railway line

Both bars are identical in every way.

Salt and pepper

The shakers were arranged the way you see them below, but when the photo was taken, the camera was level with the table. One shaker looks smaller than the other because it is farther from the camera.

Pages 8 – 9 Misleading Measurements

Circle size

The green circles are exactly the same size.

Rectangle comparison

The yellow rectangle is the same size as the top green rectangle.

Tabletop teaser

The two tabletops are identical in shape and size. You could trace one tabletop's shape onto a piece of paper and lay it over the other one to prove it.

Pointing apart

The distance between each pair of arrow tips is identical, as a ruler will show you.

Pages 12 – 13 Two-in-One Illusions

Face the vase

This really is a picture of a vase, but it's been drawn so that its shape creates a background image of two faces in profile.

Hair or no hair?

Turn the page upside down to see the other man!

Pointing both ways

There is no correct answer to this – we could have drawn either set of arrows to produce this picture. You can probably easily see both versions.

Soda or glasses?

We drew the glasses first, but again there is no correct answer here. We designed the glasses to make the gaps look like bottles, so what you see is up to you.

Page 15 Context Illusions

Whiter than white

The paper is the same shade of white in all places.

Side by side

The paths are the same. In real life your view at any time is always from the single fixed point of where you are. This means that if two separate paths looked identical in a photograph taken from that one position, they would be different in reality. Your clever brain applies this principle to the picture, but the rules of a drawing are different than the rules of reality, leaving your brain confused.

Pages 20 – 21

Inversion Illusions

Target rings

The image should appear with black replacing white, and vice versa, when you see the ghostly image.

Traffic lights

The light blue spot appears red, the dark blue spot appears yellow, and the purple spot appears green, just like a traffic light.

Color transmission

You should see the following image:

Pages 16 – 17 Color Perception

Gray areas

There is only one shade of gray here.

Shades of color

There are only four colors here. The darker and lighter versions of each color are assumptions made by your brain based on the white and black strips that overlap the colors.

Pages 18 – 19

Color shifts

Color flood

The paper in the center of the shape is exactly the same color as the paper just outside the shape.

Boundary issues

There are actually three different shades of green. The top right quarter is darkest and the bottom left quarter is lightest. The other two quarters are an in-between shade.

Colored lights

All the center tiles are exactly the same color as the separate gray tile. Your brain is "color correcting" according to the surrounding image, which it thinks is lit by a different color light in each case. To understand this, imagine how everything would look different if you had a red light bulb in a lamp instead of a white one. Your brain is assuming that something similar is happening here, and it's adjusting so automatically to the different lighting situations that you are unable to "switch off" this behavior!

Stimulating shapes

None of these shapes are really there, and the paper doesn't change color. Still, the visual cues strongly suggest that they exist, and it's quite normal to see the paper as a slightly different color.

Page 22 Grid Illusions

Shape in the hole

There are no circles on the page, but there certainly appear to be!

Coloring circles

There are no circles, colored or not, but your brain thinks there are.

Index

About the Author

Dr. Gareth Moore is the author of a wide range of puzzle and brain-training books for both children and adults, including *The Kids' Book of Puzzles, The Mammoth Book of Brain Games,* and *The Rough Guide Book of Brain Training.* He is also the founder of daily brain training site **www.BrainedUp.com**. He earned his Ph.D from Cambridge University (UK) in the field of computer speech recognition, teaching machines to understand spoken words.